Frank Philemon

Field Research Strategies

FIELD RESEARCH STRATEGIES

WRITTEN BY: Frank Philemon
P.O. Box, 116,
LIWALE-LINDI
TANZANIA
+255762426746
naxfra@gmail.com
  © 2016

CONTENTS

ACKNOWLEDGEMENT

This book is a result of the direct and indirect effort and contribution of many people in which I sincerely do admit their effort in the motivating passionate and persistence by contributing the work of this book. I thank a lot the members of academic staff especially the department of geography at Liwale High School for their challenging ideas that developed this book.

I also extend my gratitude to the Heavenly Almighty God for His protection and blessings to my life. Other special thanks I extend to my lovely wife Mariam Lucas and students at Liwale high school as well as Naxfra Mixed Education Enrichment for extending their hearts and hands so as to cooperate with me in accomplishing the work of this book.

Amazon Company is the last but the least. Thank you for sacrificing your comfort and rights the greater good. God bless you all the individuals who have in their personal and official capacity, contributed in one way or another for realization of this book are sincerely acknowledge; without your effort this book would not be accomplished.

PREFACE

"Field Research Strategies" is the book developed through maximization of simplification of basic concepts about aspects of Research. This makes its content easily accessible to all geographers (Researcher) and students in secondary schools, high schools, colleges and universities.

This book has been written with the strong aim of helping geographers and alike in getting in-depth understanding and improving their knowledge and skills in all issues of research. The author is confident that this book will be an invaluable asset for schools, colleges and universities and that students as well as teachers and lecturers will find it useful in making the teaching and learning process easier, pleasant and more fruitful.

Any efforts and contribution in one way or another incurred by all people so as to accomplish the work of this book is acknowledged; without their support this book would not have been written and seen by all of the people of the universe. I acknowledge all writers that I used their books as references to complete the work of this book.

Frank Philemon
naxfra@gmail.com
© 2016

DEDICATION

This book I dedicate to my hero and so much beloved mother; **Coretha Karol** in her great and strong support on my life. She cared and given me the opportunity to go to school, so as to pave the way for my life. Dear mom, I won't ever forget your heroines in my all living life.

Field Research Strategies

CHAPTER ONE

RESEARCH BACKGROUND

By definition, research is the systematic search and collection of information on a specific field of knowlegde or it is the systematic process of collecting information and interpleting them. In other way, research can be defined as a scientific and systematic search for pertinent information on a specific topic.

Characteristics of Research.
The following are qualities and characteristics of a good or scientific research:

1. *Research is systematic:* There are rules and procedures in conducting research e.g. identifying the problems, methods etc.

2. *Research is logical*: Involves of reasoning and judging idea

3. *Research is empirical:* Research is based on empirical evidence or observable data.

4. *Research is replicable:* Replicability in a new research can be done when other researches that has been done previonsly to see wheather they obtained the same result.

5. *Research is generative:* This is one of the most valuable characeteristics of research because answering one question led to generating of many other new questions.

6. *Research is refutable:* Advices through the process of obligation which involves submitting personal knowledge with empirical test that allows personal knowledge to be refuted.

7. *Research is scientific:* Based on empirical evidence with carefully designed study.

Motives for Undertaking Research
The possible motives for doing research may be more of the following:
1. Desire to get a research degree along with its consequential benefits;
2. Desire to face the challenge in solving the unsolved problems, i.e., concern over practical
3. problems initiates research;
4. Desire to get intellectual joy of doing some creative work;
5. Desire to be of service to society;
6. Desire to get respectability.

However, this is not an exhaustive list of factors motivating people to undertake research studies. Many more factors such as directives of government, employment conditions, curiosity about new things, desire to understand causal relationships, social thinking and awakening, and the like may as well motivate (or at times compel) people to perform research operations.

Research and Scientific Method
For a clear perception of the term research, one should know the meaning of scientific method. The two terms, research and scientific method, are closely related. Research can be termed as "an inquiry into the nature of, the reasons for, and the consequences of any particular set of circumstances, whether these circumstances are experimentally controlled or recorded just as they occur. Further, research implies the researcher is interested in more than particular results; he is interested in the repeatability of the results and in their extension to more complicated and general situations."

On the other hand, the philosophy common to all research methods and techniques, although they may vary considerably from one science to another, is usually given the name of scientific method. In this context, Karl Pearson writes, "The scientific method is one and same in the branches (of science) and that method is the method of all logically trained minds … the

11

unity of all sciences consists alone in its methods, not its material; the man who classifies facts of any kind whatever, who sees their mutual relation and describes their sequences, is applying the Scientific Method and is a man of science."

Scientific method is the pursuit of truth as determined by logical considerations. The ideal of science is to achieve a systematic interrelation of facts. Scientific method attempts to achieve "this ideal by *experimentation, observation, logical arguments* from accepted postulates and a combination of these three in varying proportions."

In scientific method, logic aids in formulating propositions explicitly and accurately so that their possible alternatives become clear. Further, logic develops the consequences of such alternatives, and when these are compared with observable phenomena, it becomes possible for the researcher or the scientist to state which alternative is most in harmony with the observed facts. All this is done through experimentation and survey investigations which constitute the integral parts of scientific method. Experimentation is done to test hypotheses and to discover new relationships.

But the conclusions drawn on the basis of experimental data are generally criticized for faulty assumptions, poorly designed experiments, badly executed experiments or faulty interpretations. As such the researcher must pay all possible attention while developing the experimental design and must state only probable inferences. The purpose of survey investigations may also be to provide scientifically gathered information to work as a basis for the researchers for their conclusions.

The scientific method is, thus, based on certain basic postulates which can be stated as under:
1. It relies on empirical evidence;
2. It utilizes relevant concepts;
3. It is committed to only objective considerations;
4. It presupposes ethical neutrality, i.e., it aims at nothing but making only adequate and correct statements about population objects;

12

5. It results into probabilistic predictions;
6. Its methodology is made known to all concerned for critical scrutiny are for use in testing the conclusions through replication;
7. It aims at formulating most general axioms or what can be termed as scientific theories.

Purposes or objectives of Research:
1) To generate new knowledge.
2) To gain deeper understanding of the phenomena.
3) To provide accurately characteristics or features to a particular individual situation on an event.
4) To find answers to unanswered problems.
5) To determine whether the data collected at one point in time can predict even all behaviours that occurs in the data point in time.
6) To include intervention where some research seek to determine whether the phenomenon can be improved or controlled by a particular intervention.
7) To improve human activities for the betterment of people.

Significance, Uses, Importance or Advantages of Research:
(i) Helps to know the reality of study.
(ii) Enable to solve different problem in a certain area.
(iii) Facilitate in promoting development of logical thinking of a person.
(iv) Helps to add knowledge to existing knowledge.
(v) It develops source of income.
(vi) Also uses as the tools for providing reliable information.
(vii) Provide acurate solution to the problems.
(vii) Enable the members of the society to be well infomed about their social surrounding.

Problems of Reseach or Disadvantages of Research:
(i) Research is expensive and require a lot of money which may lack.
(ii) Research is time consuming, because it involves long process.
(iii) Researchers may encounter problems such as language barrier and insecurity.

(iv) Large amount of data may appear unnecessary and confuse the researchers.

(v) Research needs expert knowledge about research technique, hence one need to be trained.

(vi) Needs a researcher to study a wide range of literature and techniques before conducting research.

Quality of a Good Research.

There are two necessary conditions of a good research which are used to judge the quality of the research:

(i) Validity

(ii) Reliability

01. *Validity:* Validity refers to the appropriateness, meaningfullness, and usefullness of the instrunment. Forexample, you can not get a right data of intelligent students without using intelligency test.

02. *Reliability:* Refers to the consistency or repeatability of instrument. Even other reserchers should come with the same result asthe former researcher found.

Frank Philemon

CHAPTER TWO

TYPES OF RESEARCH

Classification of research depends on the *Purpose of research* and *Approach to be used in a research*. The following are the main types of research where others originated from:
  (i) Basic research
  (ii) Applied research
  (iii) Evaluative research.

1. ***Basic Reseaech:*** A basic research also known as *fundamental research*. By definition, basic research is the research in which provides a fundamental body of knowledge. It is concerned on the foundation of the theory or contribution of the existing body of knowledge (to add knowledge).

2. ***Applied Research:*** By definition; applied research referred to the research that conducted to solve an immediate problems. Also, appplied research referred as *action research*. Action research, depend to the extent which the research is directed towards the solution of problems.

3. ***Evaluative Research***: Evaluative research is the research that attempt to assess stations of something in order to determine its level of worth.

Types of Basic (Fundamental) Research:
(1) ***Quantitative Research:*** Quantitative research deals with quantification of information. Measures numerical forms of information.
(2) ***Qualitative Research:*** It is the research that use nonquantitative (qualitative) method in studying a certain phenomena.

Types of Quantitative research:
  (a)Experimental Research: It is the research that administer two or more groups, then compare in order to determine the effectiveness of treatment.

(b)**Non Experimental Research:** The researcher in this research identify variables and look for the relationship among those variables.

Types of Qualitative Research:

(i) *Ethnograph Research:* In this research data are collected through cultural books.

(ii) *Case Study Research:* This is the research that involves indepth concentration of one individual, group, situation or extents that have been studied over time.

(iii) *Content Analysis Research:* This thype of qualitative research focus on analysis of content of the written documents.

Differences Between Qualitative and Quantitative Research:

S/N	Qualitative Research	Quantitative Research
1	Deals with description.	Deals with numbers.
2	Data can be observed but not measured.	Data can be measured eg. Height, level.
3	Interpretation based on participants.	Interpretation based on the researcher.
4	Holistic picture.	Summarized picture.
5	More subjective to describe a problem.	More objective to describe the problem.
6	Setting is natural.	Setting is artificial.
7	Deals with individual information.	Deals with generalization of informaton.
8	Possible with many tools or methods	Possible with one tools or methods
9	The key instrument is a Researcher.	The key instrument is a sample.
10	Tools are unstructured	Tools are structured.

General Types ff Research

The following are the general types of research:

17

1. **Descriptive Research:** Is the research that involves Survey and facts of finding. Tend to report about what has happened or what is happening.

2. **Applied or Action Research:** Is the research that aim at finding solution for an immediate problems facing a society or any organisation. Concerned to some natural phenomena or related to pure mathematic.

3. **Analytical Research:** This is the research which uses the information that already available. It make the critical evaluation of materials.

4. **Quantitative Research:** It is the research that based on mesurement of quantity or amount. Deals with numerical forms.

5. **Qualitative Reseacrh:** Is the kind of research that aim to discover the underlying motives and desire for the purpose. It involves quality or kind.

6. **Conceptual Research:** Is the research which deals with abstract ideas, priciples or theory. Used by philosophers and thinkers to develop new concept or to interprete the exisiting ones.

7. **Empirical Research:** This relies on experience and observation alone rather than theory. It is data based and experimental based research. Also it is known as *experimental research.*

CHAPTER THREE

SOURCES OF DATA IN RESEARCH

Data are information, especially facts collected to be examined and considered or to be used in decision making or different purposes. There are two main sources of data in research:
  (i) Primary source of data
  (ii) Secondary source of data

Primary source of data: Are data collected from the field which are original data. Are first hand data (first hand obtained data) that collected through observation, interview, quationnaires among others.

Secondary seource of data: Are data that obtained from other people's findings. Obtained from various records like text books, journals, films, magazine, maps, statistical abstract and so on.

Collecting the Data
Data at hand are inadequate, and hence, it is necessary to collect data that are appropriate. There are several ways of collecting the appropriate data which differ considerably in context of money costs, time and other resources at the disposal of the researcher.

Primary data can be collected either through experiment or through survey. If the researcher conducts an experiment, he observes some quantitative measurements, or the data, with the help of which he examines the truth contained in his hypothesis. But in the case of a survey, data can be collected by any one or more of the following ways:

(i) *By observation:* This method implies the collection of information by way of investigator's own observation, without interviewing the respondents. The information obtained relates to what is currently happening and is not complicated by either the past behaviour or future intentions or attitudes of respondents.

This method is no doubt an expensive method and the information provided by this method is also very limited. As such this method is not suitable in inquiries where large samples are concerned.

(ii) *Through personal interview:* The investigator follows a rigid procedure and seeks answers to a set of pre-conceived questions through personal interviews. This method of collecting data is usually carried out in a structured way where output depends upon the ability of the interviewer to a large extent.

(iii) *Through telephone interviews:* This method of collecting information involves contacting the respondents on telephone itself. This is not a very widely used method but it plays an important role in industrial surveys in developed regions, particularly, when the survey has to be accomplished in a very limited time.

(iv) *By mailing of questionnaires:* The researcher and the respondents do come in contact with each other if this method of survey is adopted. Questionnaires are mailed to the respondents with a request to return after completing the same. It is the most extensively used method in various economic and business surveys.

Before applying this method, usually a Pilot Study for testing the questionnaire is conducted to reveals the weaknesses, if any, of the questionnaire. Questionnaire to be used must be prepared very carefully so that it may prove to be effective in collecting the relevant information.

(v) *Through schedules:* Under this method the enumerators are appointed and given training. They are provided with schedules containing relevant questions. These enumerators go to respondents with these schedules. Data are collected by filling up the schedules by enumerators on the basis of replies given by respondents. Much depends upon the capability of enumerators so far as this method is concerned. Some occasional field checks on the work of the enumerators may ensure sincere work.

Collection of Secondary Data

Secondary data means data that are already available i.e., they refer to the data which have already been collected and analysed by someone else. When the researcher utilizes secondary data, then he has to look into various sources from where he can obtain them. In this case he is certainly not confronted with the problems that are usually associated with the collection of original data.

Secondary data may either be published data or unpublished data. Usually published data are available in:

a) Various publications of the central, state are local governments;

b) Various publications of foreign governments or of international bodies and their subsidiary organisations;

c) Technical and trade journals;

d) Books, magazines and newspapers;

e) Reports and publications of various associations connected with business and industry, banks, stock exchanges, etc.;

f) Reports prepared by research scholars, universities, economists, etc. in different fields; and

g) Public records and statistics, historical documents, and other sources of published information.

The sources of unpublished data are many; they may be found in diaries, letters, unpublished biographies and autobiographies and also may be available with scholars and research workers, trade associations, labour bureaus and other public/ private individuals and organisations.

Researcher must be very careful in using secondary data. He must make a minute scrutiny because it is just possible that the secondary data may be unsuitable or may be inadequate in the context of the problem which the researcher wants to study. By way of caution, the researcher, before using secondary data, must see that they possess the following characteristics:

1. Reliability of data: The reliability can be tested by finding out such things about the said data:

a) Who collected the data?

b) What were the sources of data?
c) Were they collected by using proper methods?
d) At what time were they collected?
e) Was there any bias of the compiler?
f) What level of accuracy was desired? Was it achieved?

2. Suitability of data: The data that are suitable for one enquiry may not necessarily be found suitable in another enquiry. Hence, if the available data are found to be unsuitable, they should not be used by the researcher. In this context, the researcher must very carefully scrutinize the definition of various terms and units of collection used at the time of collecting the data from the primary source originally.

Similarly, the object, scope and nature of the original enquiry must also be studied. If the researcher finds differences in these, the data will remain unsuitable for the present enquiry and should not be used.

3. Adequacy of data: If the level of accuracy achieved in data is found inadequate for the purpose of the present enquiry, they will be considered as inadequate and should not be used by the researcher. The data will also be considered inadequate, if they are related to an area which may be either narrower or wider than the area of the present enquiry. From all this we can say that it is very risky to use the already available data.

The already available data should be used by the researcher only when he finds them reliable, suitable and adequate. But he should not blindly discard the use of such data if they are readily available from authentic sources and are also suitable and adequate for in that case it will not be economical to spend time and energy in field surveys for collecting information. At times, there may be wealth of usable information in the already available data which must be used by an intelligent researcher but with due precaution.

Field Research Strategies

CHAPTER FOUR

STAGES IN RESEARCH

Stages in research are steps, process or cyclic of research. Research process consists of series of actions or steps necessary to effectively carry out research and the desired sequencing of these steps. How does one go about developing working hypotheses? The answer is by using the following approach:

a) Discussions with colleagues and experts about the problem, its origin and the objectives in seeking a solution,

b) Examination of data and records, if available, concerning the problem for possible trends, peculiarities and other clues,

c) Review of similar studies in the area or of the studies on similar problems; and

d) Exploratory personal investigation which involves original field interviews on a limited scale with interested parties and individuals with a view to secure greater insight into the practical aspects of the problem.

Research as a Systematic Process, Should be Structured in Stages:

Stage 1: Identification of The Problem: Problem identification is the question or idea of a researcher which ought to be answered through data collection. This stage involves the problems to be investigated.

Stage 2: Formulation of Hypothesis: Formulation of hypothesis is the form of prediction or forecasting. Is like an outcome or explaination of the future result.

Stage 3: *Literature Review:* Literature review is an informtion obtained from what others say on the same problems. Obtained from other researches and writtings or documents.

Stage 4: *Selecting Research Design:* It involves the designation of or on the study like designing participants (population) or number of people to be involved in the (sample size) study and location of the study as well as accessbitity to the field area. Uses quantitative and qualitative approach.

Stage 5: *Developing the Research Instrument:* Research instruments means tools to be used by the researcher in the field to collect information. Tools can be interviews, observation, checklist, questionnaire among others.

Stage 6: *Data Collection:* Data collection involves the administration or administrating the instruments. This done when a researcher is currently and present in the field.

Stage 7: *Data Analysis:* Data analysis involves of putting the collected data or information into sensible ideas to answer the quaestions. Also known as information analysis.

Stage 8: *Report Writing:* Report writing involves carefully formulation of coclution and generalization as well as recommendation of the research. This stage a researcher communicate with the public through his or her finding(s).

CHAPTER FIVE

RESEARCH PROBLEM

A research problem, in general, refers to some difficulty which a researcher experiences in the context of either a theoretical or practical situation and wants to obtain a solution for them.

Selecting the Problem

The research problem undertaken for study must be carefully selected. The task is a difficult one, although it may not appear to be so. Help may be taken from a research guide in this connection. Nevertheless, every researcher must find out his own salvation for research problems cannot be borrowed.

A problem must spring from the researcher's mind like a plant springing from its own seed. Thus, a research guide can at the most only help a researcher choose a subject. However, the following points may be observed by a researcher in selecting a research problem or a subject for research:

(i) Subject which is overdone should not be normally chosen, for it will be a difficult task to throw any new light in such a case.

(ii) Controversial subject should not become the choice of an average researcher.

(iii) Too narrow or too vague problems should be avoided.

(iv) The subject selected for research should be familiar and feasible so that the related research material or sources of research are within one's reach.

(v) The importance of the subject, the qualifications and the training of a researcher, the costs involved, and the time factor are few other criteria that must also be considered in selecting a problem. In other words, before

28

the final selection of a problem is done, a researcher must ask himself the following questions:

     a. Whether he is well equipped in terms of his background to carry out the research?

     b. Whether the study falls within the budget he can afford?

     c. Whether the necessary cooperation can be obtained from those who must participate in research as subjects?

If the answers to all these questions are in the affirmative, one may become sure so far as the practicability of the study is concerned.

(vi) The selection of a problem must be preceded by a preliminary study. This may not be necessary when the problem requires the conduct of a research closely similar to one that has already been done. But when the field of inquiry is relatively new and does not have available a set of well-developed techniques, a brief feasibility study must always be undertaken.

If the subject for research is selected properly by observing the above mentioned points, the research will not be a boring drudgery, rather it will be love's labour. In fact, zest for work is a must. The subject or the problem selected must involve the researcher and must have an upper most place in his mind so that he may undertake all pains needed for the study.

Necessity of Defining the Problem

"A problem clearly stated is a problem half solved". This statement signifies the need for defining a research problem. The problem to be investigated must be defined unambiguously for that will help to discriminate relevant data from the irrelevant ones.

A proper definition of research problem will enable the researcher to be on the track whereas an ill-defined problem may create hurdles. Questions like:

   * What data are to be collected?

   * What characteristics of data are relevant and need to be studied?

   * What relations are to be explored?

   * What techniques are to be used for the purpose?

29

Thus, defining a research problem properly is a prerequisite for any study and is a step of the highest importance. In fact, formulation of a problem is often more essential than its solution. It is only on careful detailing the research problem that we can work out the research design and can smoothly carry on all the consequential steps involved while doing research.

Technique Involved in Defining a Problem

Defining a problem involves the task of laying down boundaries within which a researcher shall study the problem with a pre-determined objective in view. However, defining a problem it is a task that must be tackled intelligently to avoid the perplexity encountered in a research operation.

The usual approach is that the researcher should himself pose a question and set-up techniques and procedures for throwing light on the question concerned for formulating or defining the research problem. But such an approach generally does not produce definitive results because the question phrased in such a fashion is usually in broad general terms and as such may not be in a form suitable for testing.

The research problem should be defined in a systematic manner, giving due weightage to all relating points. The technique for the purpose involves the undertaking of the following steps generally one after the other:

(i) Statement of the problem in a general way,
(ii) Understanding the nature of the problem,
 (iii) Surveying the available literature,
(iv) Developing the ideas through discussions, and
(v) Rephrasing the research problem into a working proposition.

(i) Statement of the problem in a general way: First of all the problem should be stated in a broad general way, keeping in view either some practical concern or some scientific or intellectual interest. For this purpose, the researcher must immerse himself thoroughly in the subject matter concerning which he wishes to pose a problem.

In case of social research, it is considered advisable to do some field observation and as such the researcher may undertake some sort of preliminary survey or what is often called *pilot survey*. Then the researcher can himself state the problem or he can seek the guidance of the guide or the subject expert in accomplishing this task. Often, the guide puts forth the problem in general terms, and it is then up to the researcher to narrow it down and phrase the problem in operational terms.

In case there is some directive from an organisational authority, the problem then can be stated accordingly. The problem stated in a broad general way may contain various ambiguities which must be resolved by cool thinking and rethinking over the problem. At the same time the feasibility of a particular solution has to be considered and the same should be kept in view while stating the problem.

(ii) Understanding the nature of the problem: The next step in defining the problem is to understand its origin and nature clearly. The best way of understanding the problem is to discuss it with those who first raised it in order to find out how the problem originally came about and with what objectives in view. If the researcher has stated the problem himself, he should consider once again all those points that induced him to make a general statement concerning the problem.

For a better understanding of the nature of the problem involved, he can enter into discussion with those who have a good knowledge of the problem concerned or similar other problems. The researcher should also keep in view the environment within which the problem is to be studied and understood.

(iii) Surveying the available literature: All available literature concerning the problem at hand must necessarily be surveyed and examined before a definition of the research problem is given. This means that the researcher must be well-conversant with relevant theories in the field, reports and records as also all other relevant literature. He must devote sufficient time in reviewing of research already undertaken on related problems.

31

This is done to find out what data and other materials, if any, are available for operational purposes. "Knowing what data are available often serves to narrow the problem itself as well as the technique that might be used." This would also help a researcher to know if there are certain gaps in the theories, or whether the existing theories applicable to the problem under study are inconsistent with each other, or whether the findings of the different studies do not follow a pattern consistent with the theoretical expectations and so on.

All this will enable a researcher to take new strides in the field for furtherance of knowledge i.e., he can move up starting from the existing premise. Studies on related problems are useful for indicating the type of difficulties that may be encountered in the present study as also the possible analytical shortcomings. At times such studies may also suggest useful and even new lines of approach to the present problem.

(iv) Developing the ideas through discussions: Discussion concerning a problem often produces useful information. Various new ideas can be developed through such an exercise. Hence, a researcher must discuss his problem with his colleagues and others who have enough experience in the same area or in working on similar problems. This is quite often known as an *experience survey*.

People with rich experience are in a position to enlighten the researcher on different aspects of his proposed study and their advice and comments are usually invaluable to the researcher. They help him sharpen his focus of attention on specific aspects within the field. Discussions with such persons should not only be confined to the formulation of the specific problem at hand, but should also be concerned with the general approach to the given problem, techniques that might be used, possible solutions, etc.

(v) Rephrasing the research problem: Finally, the researcher must sit to rephrase the research problem into a working proposition. Once the nature of the problem has been clearly understood, the environment (within which the problem has got to be studied) has been defined, discussions

over the problem have taken place and the available literature has been surveyed and examined, rephrasing the problem into analytical or operational terms is not a difficult task. Through rephrasing, the researcher puts the research problem in as specific terms as possible so that it may become operationally viable and may help in the development of working hypotheses.

In addition to what has been stated above, the following points must also be observed while defining a research problem:

    a. Technical terms and words or phrases, with special meanings used in the statement of the problem, should be clearly defined.

    b. Basic assumptions or postulates (if any) relating to the research problem should be clearly stated.

    c. A straight forward statement of the value of the investigation (i.e., the criteria for the selection of the problem) should be provided.

    d. The suitability of the time-period and the sources of data available must also be considered by the researcher in defining the problem.

    e. The scope of the investigation or the limits within which the problem is to be studied must be mentioned explicitly in defining a research problem.

Field Research Strategies

CHAPTER SIX

RESEARCH HYPOTHESIS

Hypothesis by definition refers to the prediction about the study of outcome. Hypothesis is the tentative prediction of outcome or result. Hypothes is also defined as the scientific guess of the outcome of interest. A good hypothesis must possess the following characteristics:

(i) Hypothesis should be clear and precise. If the hypothesis is not clear and precise, the inferences drawn on its basis cannot be taken as reliable.

(ii) Hypothesis should be capable of being tested. In a swamp of untestable hypotheses, many a time the research programmes have bogged down. Some prior study may be done by researcher in order to make hypothesis a testable one. A hypothesis "is testable if other deductions can be made from it which, in turn, can be confirmed or disproved by observation."

(iii) Hypothesis should state relationship between variables, if it happens to be a relational hypothesis.

(iv) Hypothesis should be limited in scope and must be specific. A researcher must remember that narrower hypotheses are generally more testable and he should develop such hypotheses.

(v) Hypothesis should be stated as far as possible in most simple terms so that the same is easily understandable by all concerned. But one must remember that simplicity of hypothesis has nothing to do with its significance.

(vi) Hypothesis should be amenable to testing within a reasonable time. One should not use even an excellent hypothesis, if the same cannot be tested in reasonable time for one cannot spend a life-time collecting data to test it.

(vii) Hypothesis must explain the facts that gave rise to the need for explanation. This means that by using the hypothesis plus other known and

35

accepted generalizations, one should be able to deduce the original problem condition. Thus hypothesis must actually explain what it claims to explain; it should have empirical reference.

(viii) Hypothesis should be consistent with most known facts i.e., it must be consistent with a substantial body of established facts. In other words, it should be one which judges accept as being the most likely.

Types of research hypothesis
There are only two hypothesis in research as namely below:
    a) Altenative hypothesis,
    b) Null hypothesis.

*(a)***Altenative Hypothesis***:* Is the hypothesis that stated in a positive way. Also it is known as *positive hypothesis*. For example; there is a relationship between mass failure of secondary school students and shortage of teachers to the school.

(b)   Null Hypothesis: Null hypothesis is stated in a negative way. It is also known as *negative hypothesis*. For example; there is no relationship between mass failure of secondary school students and the shortage of teachers to the schools.

Brief Explanation on Hypothesis
The *null hypothesis* and the *alternative hypothesis* are chosen before the sample is drawn (the researcher must avoid the error of deriving hypotheses from the data that he collects and then testing the hypotheses from the same data). In the choice of null hypothesis, the following considerations are usually kept in view:

(a) Alternative hypothesis is usually the one which one wishes to prove and the null hypothesis is the one which one wishes to disprove. Thus, a null hypothesis represents the hypothesis we are trying to reject, and alternative hypothesis represents all other possibilities.

(b) If the rejection of a certain hypothesis when it is actually true involves great risk, it is taken as null hypothesis because then the probability of rejecting it when it is true is a (the level of significance) which is chosen very small.

(c) Null hypothesis should always be specific hypothesis i.e., it should not state about or approximately a certain value. Generally, in hypothesis testing we proceed on the basis of null hypothesis, keeping the alternative hypothesis in view. Why so? The answer is that on the assumption that null hypothesis is true, one can assign the probabilities to different possible sample results, but this cannot be done if we proceed with the alternative hypothesis. Hence the use of null hypothesis (at times also known as statistical hypothesis) is quite frequent.

(d) *The level of significance:* This is a very important concept in the context of hypothesis testing. It is always some percentage (usually 5%) which should be chosen with great care, thought and reason.

Importance of Hypothesis:
(i) Guide researchers by limiting area of research
(ii) It indicates the type of data required
(iii) It defines which facts are relevant and which are not.
(iv) It determines the most appropriate techniques of data analysis
(v) It contributes to theory development

Field Research Strategies

CHAPTER SEVEN

RESEARCH DESIGN

The design is the structure of any scientific work. Research design refers to the plan of structure of a research work. A research design is the arrangement of conditions for collection and analysis of data in a manner that aims to combine relevance to the research purpose with economy in procedure. Research design gives direction and systematizes the research different types of research designs have different advantages and disadvantages.

The formidable problem that follows the task of defining the research problem is the preparation of the design of the research project, popularly known as the "research design". Decisions regarding what, where, when, how much, by what means concerning an inquiry or a research study constitute a research design.

In fact, the research design is the conceptual structure within which research is conducted; it constitutes the blueprint for the collection, measurement and analysis of data. As such the design includes an outline of what the researcher will do from writing the hypothesis and its operational implications to the final analysis of data. More explicitly, the dosing decisions happen to be in respect of:
  a) What is the study about?
  b) Why is the study being made?
  c) Where will the study be carried out?
  d) What type of data is required?
  e) Where can the required data be found?
  f) What periods of time will the study include?
  g) What will be the sample design?
  h) What techniques of data collection will be used?
  i) How will the data be analysed?
  j) In what style will the report be prepared?

Keeping in view the stated design decisions; one may split the overall research design into the following parts:

1) *The sampling design* which deals with the method of selecting items to be observed for the given study,

2) *The observational design* which relates to the conditions under which the observations are to be made,

3) *The statistical design* which concerns with the question of how many items are to be observed and how the information and data gathered are to be analysed and

4) *The operational design* which deals with the techniques by which the procedures specified in the sampling, statistical and observational designs can be carried out.

From what has been stated above, we can state the important features of a research design as under:

(i) It is a plan that specifies the sources and types of information relevant to the research problem.

(ii) It is a strategy specifying which approach will be used for gathering and analysing the data.

(iii) It also includes the time and cost budgets since most studies are done under these two constraints.

In Brief, Research Design Must, at least, Contain:
  (a) A clear statement of the research problem,
  (b) Procedures and techniques to be used for gathering information,
  (c) The population to be studied and
  (d) Methods to be used in processing and analysing data.

The preparation of the research design, appropriate for a particular research problem, involves usually the consideration of the following:

(i)   The means of obtaining the information,

(ii)   The availability and skills of the researcher and his staff,

(iii)   Explanation of the way in which selected means of obtaining information will be organized and the reasoning leading to the selection,

(iv)   The time available for research and

(v)   The cost factor relating to research, i.e., the finance available for the purpose.

Features of a Good Research Design

A good design is often characterized by adjectives like flexible, appropriate, efficient, economical and so on. Generally, the design which minimizes bias and maximizes the reliability of the data collected and analyzed is considered a good design. The design which gives the smallest experimental error is supposed to be the best design in many investigations.

Similarly, a design which yields maximal information and provides an opportunity for considering many different aspects of a problem is considered most appropriate and efficient design in respect of many research problems. Thus, the question of good design is related to the purpose or objective of the research problem and also with the nature of the problem to be studied.

A design may be quite suitable in one case, but may be found wanting in one respect or the other in the context of some other research problem. One single design cannot serve the purpose of all types of research problems. A research design appropriate for a particular research problem, usually involves the consideration of the following factors:

(i)The means of obtaining information,

(ii) The availability and skills of the researcher and his staff, if any,

(iii) The objective of the problem to be studied,

(iv) The nature of the problem to be studied and

(v) The availability of time and money for the research work.

CHAPTER EIGHT

DATA COLLECTION IN RESEARCH

Data collection in research deploy some ways which are called methods, tools, instrunments, or techniques of data collection in research. There are many methods which are, used to collect data. Some and the main of them are:

a) Observation,
b) Interview,
c) Checklist view,
d) Documentary review,
e) Quationnaires,
f) Experimentation,
g) Focus group discussion and
h) Schedules.

Note: In this book, the following methods of data collection are only goind to be described: Interview, Quetionnaires, Observation, Schedule and Focus group discusion.

Selection of Appropriate Method for Data Collection:
1. Nature, scope and object of enquiry: This constitutes the most important factor affecting the choice of a particular method. The method selected should be such that it suits the type of enquiry that is to be conducted by the researcher. This factor is also important in deciding whether the data already available (secondary data) are to be used or the data not yet available (primary data) are to be collected.

2. Availability of funds: Availability of funds for the research project determines to a large extent the method to be used for the collection of data. When funds at the disposal of the researcher are very limited, he will have to select a comparatively cheaper method which may not be as efficient and effective as some other costly method. Finance, in fact, is a big constraint in practice and the researcher has to act within this limitation.

3. Time factor: Availability of time has also to be taken into account in deciding a particular method of data collection. Some methods take relatively more time, whereas with others the data can be collected in a comparatively shorter duration. The time at the disposal of the researcher, thus, affects the selection of the method by which the data are to be collected.

4. Precision required: Precision required is yet another important factor to be considered at the time of selecting the method of collection of data.

01.   Observation Method Of Data Collection.

Observation refers to the direct evidence of the eye to witness the evidence. It is the method of data collection that involves eyes to witness the events.

Advantages of Observation method:
   (i) First hand information can be collected easily.
   (ii) It saves time as one does not have a look for data else where.
   (iii) The method allow participation of the researcher on the environment.
   (iv) Does not allow information modification.
   (v)The method helps researcher to develop the spirit of self-reliance and self determination.
   (vi)It avoid language barrier .
   (viI) Flexible enough to be used whenever and wherever needed.

Disadvantages of Observation method:
   (i) It cost in terms of time and money in reaching the place of events.
   (ii) There some elements of biasiness in witnessing events, hence no correct information.
   (iii) Some genegraphical phenomena are not easily obtained e.g. Secret issue in the military services.
   (iv) It is subjective because, data are based on personal observation.
   (v) It can be dangerous because, it needs presence of researcher on the area of the events.
   (vi) Needs a person who have all five sense of organ.

(vii) Misinterpretation may occur due to the poor personal concentration.

Types of observation method
There are two main types of observation method:

1. Participant Observation
It is refferred as the direct observation. The researcher get to know the ideas of the group.

Advantages of participant observation:
(i) Researcher get to be familia with the environment.
(ii) Researcher get to know the ideas of the group.
(iii) Researcher become part and percel of the community.
(iv) First hand information may be collected.

Disadvantages of participant observation:
(i) Information gathered may not be complete if a researcher connot ask others to get more knowledge.
(ii) It is costly in term of time and money in reaching to the place of event to be witnessed.
(iii) Has elements of business, due to being based only on personal observation.

2. Non Participant Observation
In this type, a researcher is not the part and parcel of the community. Occurs when a researchers are aside observing the activities or events.

Merits of Non participant Observation:
 (i) The researcher is not affected emotionally with the social situation of the group.
 (ii) No interference from the researcher.
 (iii) Member observed are free to discuss the matter or issues, hence a researcher may be possible to get confidential data.

Demerits of Non participant observation:

(i) Researchers does not capture the natural context of the social life of the people (in studying).

(ii) Does not provide full information to be observed, because the observer cannot acess some information (e. g. isues based in different gender).

02. Interview Method Of Data Collection

An interview is the method of data collection which involves verbal interaction between an interviewer and an interviewee (Respondent). In this method people are asked questions directly i.e. face to face and responses are recorded.

Guidelines for Successful Interviewing

Interviewing is an art and one learns it by experience. However, the following points may be kept in view by an interviewer for eliciting the desired information:

1. Interviewer must plan in advance and should fully know the problem under consideration. He must choose a suitable time and place so that the interviewee may be at ease during the interview period. For this purpose some knowledge of the daily routine of the interviewee is essential.

2. Interviewer's approach must be friendly and informal. Initially friendly greetings in accordance with the cultural pattern of the interviewee should be exchanged and then the purpose of the interview should be explained.

3. All possible effort should be made to establish proper rapport with the interviewee; people are motivated to communicate when the atmosphere is favourable.

4. Interviewer must know that ability to listen with understanding, respect and curiosity is the gateway to communication, and hence must act accordingly during the interview. For all this, the interviewer must be intelligent and must be a man with self-restraint and self-discipline.

5. To the extent possible there should be a free-flowing interview and the questions must be well phrased in order to have full cooperation of the interviewee. But the interviewer must control the course of the interview in accordance with the objective of the study.

6. In case of big enquiries, where the task of collecting information is to be accomplished by several interviewers, there should be an interview guide to be observed by all so as to ensure reasonable uniformity in respect of all salient points in the study.

Advantages of interview:
   (i) Here the researcher (interviewer) get data quickly on the spot.
   (ii) It is not restricted to both literate and illiterate people.
   (iii) Personal information can be obtained.
   (iv) It allow interaction between two sides. The side of interviewer and respondents.
   (v) The method is more flexible, and simple to change the questions depending to the situation.
   (vi) Allow high response rate through dialogue.

Disadvantages of interview.
   (i) The method is time consuming through getting and reaching respondents in the field.
   (ii) Respondents tend to be subjective because they respond by basing on their own feellings.
   (iii) It is costly because researcher have to travel to meet the respondents in the field.
   (iv) Require a high level of knowledge in interviewing. So as the interviewer to avoid biaceness.
   (v) Interviews involves small sample because they are time consuming hence few sample and data can be collected.
   (vi) Informations may be influenced by the respondent (e.g. poor community).
   (vii) The method produces non standardised responses.

(viii) Not applicable to the dumb and deaf, hence the method is subjective to some people only.

Types of interview
There are two main types of interview:
    (1) Structure interview
    (2) Unstructure interview

1. Unstructured interview
The researcher introduce the topic or theme and let the respondents to develop there ideas. Allow the interviewee to speak their ideas. No limitation to the discussion of the topic.

Merits of Unstructured interview:
    a) It is flexible because there is no restriction.
    b) More information can be revealed due to high degree of freedom.
    c) Respondentr are free to expose out their ideas and feelings.

Demerits of Unstructured interview:
    a) Difficult to compare the answers because many questions and answers are provided from different respondents.
    b) It is time consuming because, the method is not structured to get specific answers.
    c) If is not controlled or planned, may led to the irrelevance information.

2. Structured interview
This type involves structured and semi-structured form of questions asked orally. Here, this interview, the researcher or interviewer has a predetermined quaestions (prepared questions).

Weakness of structured interviews:
    a) It is not flexible, because researcher can not ask more questions outside of those prepared before.
    b) Some hidden information cannot be obtained easily.

Strength structured interview:
   (i) A researcher can compare answers from different respondent to see their validity (sameness).
   (ii) It is possible to use qualitative analysis to analyze data.
   (iii) It is not time consuming, because there are systematic prepared oral questions.

Rule or Procedures of Conducting Interview
In conducting the interview, the researcher or interviewer should have to:
   a) Create a friendly atmosphere (where the two can talk easily)
   b) Instil confidence and trust to the information will be provided by the respondents.
   c) Avoid interprenting the respondent.
   d) Avoid tape-recording as it might discourage the respondent to be free.
   e) Be neutral and should not suggest any answer.

Rules Partaining To Interviewer
Some have already in Guidelines for Successful Interviewing:
   a) The interviewer must be pleasant in any kind of iformation.
   b) Interviewer should be relaxed and friendly.
   c) The interviewer should be very familiar with the interview.
   d) The enterviewr should interact with the respondents.
   e) The interviewer shold pretest the interview guide before conducting the enterview.
   f) The interviewer should not ask leading and personal questions.
   g) The interviewer should inform the respondent about confidentiality.
   h) The interviewer should inform the respondent about and when the enterview will be conducted.

03.   Quetionnaires Method of Data Collection.
   This is the method used in data collection which consist a list of questions related to the topic.

Advantages of quationnaires:
   (1) Data can be collected as first hand.

(2) A researcher get a lot information from many respondent in a different areas.

(3) Omission of names, make respondends easily to respond to the quationnaires given.

(4) It saves time, because many questions can be handed to many respondents at the same time.

(5) Gives accurate to gauge the answers.

(6) Used in extracting many information in a broad field.

Disadvantages of quationnaires:

a) Used for only literate people and not suitable to the illiterate ones

b) Sometimes the questions may not be understood to the respondents.

c) It is costly in printing and typing quationnaires.

d) Posted quationnaires may not be received by respondents or returned back to researcher in a right time.

e) It is inappropriate where there is language barrier between the researcher and the repondent.

f) The questions may not be understood, hence the respondent will answer the way they understand.

g) There is low response rate when the respondents may not like to answer the questions.

h) It is time consuming when it covers large area and large sample size to be reached.

Types of questionnaires.

There are two main types of questions that are used in questionnaires:

a) Structured or closed ended quationnaire

b) Unstructured or open ended questionnaire

(a) Structured or Closed ended quationnaires

These are type of questions that accompanied by a list of all posible altenatives from which respondents select the answer that best desdribes their situation.

Example; (i) What type of transport do you use (circle to the best answer answer)?

(A)   Feet (B) Bicycle (C) Car (D) Aircraft
(ii) The main crops grown in Mwanza is ...
(A)   Maize (B) Cotton (C) Patatoes (D) Beanz

Advantages of Closed Ended Quationnaires:
(i) These are easier to administer and analyze because each item is followed by altenative answers.
(ii) They are economical to use both interms of money and time (no time and moneyconsuming).

Disadvantages of Structured Quationnaires:
(i) Are more difficult to construct, since categories must be well selected.
(ii) Responses are limited (should write the only given altenative).
(iii) Respondents are required to answer questions according to what the researcher's choice.

(b) Unstructured or Open Ended Quationnaires
This refers to the questions that gives the respondents complete freedom of responces that permit an individual to respond in his or her own words.

Example;
(i) How do you keep records of your monthly expenditure in your family?
(ii) What subjects do you most like in your combination?
(iii) Which one of these subjects do you consider to be important subject?

Advantages of Open Ended Quationnaires:
(i) Are simple to formulate.
(ii) Respondents are free to give out their feeling.
(iii) Permit for a great response because respondent is given personal response.
(iv) Open ended questions stimulate a person to think and give a constructive idea.

Disadvantages of Open Ended Quationnaires:
(i) Provides information which does not answer the stipulated research objective (because, respondent are free to give their opinion).
(ii) Responses given may be difficult to be analyzed.
(iii) It is time consuming due to free chance given to the respondents.

Procedures Considered in Preparing Quetionnaires:
a) The questions must be short, simple and clear straight forward.
b) The questions should be asked in a systematic manner.
c) The questions should be relevant to the topic.
d) The questions should be used polite language.
e) The questions should be free of bias.

04. Collection Of Data Through Schedules

This method of data collection is very much like the collection of data through questionnaire, with little difference which lies in the fact that schedules (pro forma containing a set of questions) are being filled in by the enumerators who are specially appointed for the purpose. These enumerators along with schedules go to respondents, put to them the questions from the pro forma in the order the questions are listed and record the replies in the space meant for the same in the pro forma.

In certain situations, schedules may be handed over to respondents and enumerators may help them in recording their answers to various questions in the said schedules. Enumerators explain the aims and objects of the investigation and also remove the difficulties which any respondent may feel in understanding the implications of a particular question or the definition or concept of difficult terms.

This method requires the selection of enumerators for filling up schedules or assisting respondents to fill up schedules and as such enumerators should be very carefully selected. The enumerators should be trained to perform their job well and the nature and scope of the investigation should be explained to them thoroughly so that they may well understand the implications of different questions put in the schedule. Enumerators should be intelligent and must possess the capacity of cross-examination in order to find out the truth. Above all, they should be honest, sincere, and hardworking and should have patience and perseverance.

This method of data collection is very useful in extensive enquiries and can lead to fairly reliable results. It is, however, very expensive and is usually adopted in investigations conducted by governmental agencies or by some big organisations. Population census all over the world is conducted through this method.

Guidelines for Constructing Questionnaire or Schedule
The researcher must pay attention to the following points in constructing an appropriate and effective questionnaire or a schedule:

1. The researcher must keep in view the problem he is to study for it provides the starting point for developing the Questionnaire or Schedule. He must be clear about the various aspects of his research problem to be dealt with in the course of his research project.

2. Appropriate form of questions depends on the nature of information sought, the sampled respondents and the kind of analysis intended. The researcher must decide whether to use closed or open-ended question. Questions should be simple and must be constructed with a view to their forming a logical part of a well thought out tabulation plan. The units of enumeration should also be defined precisely so that they can ensure accurate and full information.

3. Rough draft of the Questionnaire/Schedule is prepared, giving due thought to the appropriate sequence of putting questions. Questionnaires or schedules previously drafted (if available) may as well be looked into at this stage.

4. Researcher must invariably re-examine, and in case of need may revise the rough draft for a better one. Technical defects must be minutely scrutinized and removed.

5. Pilot study should be undertaken for pre-testing the questionnaire. The questionnaire may be edited in the light of the results of the pilot study.

6. Questionnaire must contain simple but straight forward directions for the respondents so that they may not feel any difficulty in answering the questions.

Difference between Questionnaires and Schedules
Both questionnaire and schedule are popularly used methods of collecting data in research surveys. There is much resemblance in the nature of these two methods and this fact has made many people to remark that from a practical point of view; the two methods can be taken to be the same. But from the technical point of view there is difference between the two. The important points of difference are as under:

1. The questionnaire is generally sent through mail to informants to be answered as specified in a covering letter, but otherwise without further assistance from the sender. The schedule is generally filled out by the research worker or the enumerator, who can interpret questions when necessary.

2. To collect data through questionnaire is relatively cheap and economical since we have to spend money only in preparing the questionnaire and in mailing the same to respondents. Here no field staff required. To collect data through schedules is relatively more expensive since considerable amount of money has to be spent in appointing enumerators and in importing training to them. Money is also spent in preparing schedules.

3. Non-response is usually high in case of questionnaire as many people do not respond and many return the questionnaire without answering all questions. Bias due to non-response often remains indeterminate. As against this, non-response is generally very low in case of schedules because these are filled by enumerators who are able to get answers to all questions. But there remains the danger of interviewer bias and cheating.

4. In case of questionnaire, it is not always clear as to who replies, but in case of schedule the identity of respondent is known.

5. The questionnaire method is likely to be very slow since many respondents do not return the questionnaire in time despite several reminders, but in case of schedules the information is collected well in time as they are filled in by enumerators.

6. Personal contact is generally not possible in case of the questionnaire method as questionnaires are sent to respondents by post who also in turn returns the same by post. But in case of schedules direct personal contact is established with respondents.

7. Questionnaire method can be used only when respondents are literate and cooperative, but in case of schedules the information can be gathered even when the respondents happen to be illiterate.

8. Wider and more representative distribution of sample is possible under the questionnaire method, but in respect of schedules there usually remains the difficulty in sending enumerators over a relatively wider area.

9. Risk of collecting incomplete and wrong information is relatively more under the questionnaire method, particularly when people are unable to understand questions properly. But in case of schedules, the information collected is generally complete and accurate as enumerators can remove the difficulties, if any, faced by respondents in correctly understanding the questions. As a result, the information collected through schedules is relatively more accurate than that obtained through questionnaires.

10. The success of questionnaire method lies more on the quality of the questionnaire itself, but in the case of schedules much depends upon the honesty and competence of enumerators.

11. In order to attract the attention of respondents, the physical appearance of questionnaire must be quite attractive, but this may not be

so in case of schedules as they are to be filled in by enumerators and not by respondents.

12. Along with schedules, observation method can also be used but such a thing is not possible while collecting data through questionnaires.

05. Focus Group Discassion (F.G.D)
It is the research method which involves intensive discussion on a particular issues. Normally done in a small group of people of 5 to 7 people.

Aims of Focus Group Discussion
It targets the group to get addition information, which are rendered by some talent people for the benefit of the group on the particular issues.

Advantages of focus group discussion:
(i) Researcher become active person in discussion.

(ii) Respondent get skilled of writing, and speaking as well as coordinating.

(iii) Involves low cost, because of few number of participants involved in the discussion.

(iv) Develop way of constructing ideas or points.

(v) Facilitate for a great way of exchanging of ideas.

Disadvantages of focus group discussion:
a) Very small sample size is involved.

b) Selection of group may be affected by biases or subjective due to the researcher interest and closeness of the invited participants.

c) Few respondents may dominate the discussion, especially those who are very much talkative.

d) It is difficult to analyze data collected through this method bacause many ideas can be generated and spoken out.

e) There is no equal participation because, there some people may fear to share their idea or contribution infront of the group members.

f) There is the high degree of conflict emotion among the member due to the differences in ideas and interests.

Factors Influancing for Selection of Instrunment for Data Collection.
Each instrument of data collection has streght and weakness. Factors influencing for the uses of type of instrunment for data collection, depends on the followings:

a) What you need to know?
b) Depends where the data reside on the environment.
c) Where the data is from sites.
d) Depends on resources and time availability.
e) Depends on the complement of the data to be collected.
f) Depends on frequent data collection.

Problems Hindering Data Collection In the Field:

(i) Inadequate time.
(ii) Lack of cooperation from respondents.
(iii) Inaccessible areas.
(iv) Inadequate source of data.
(v) Language barrier.
(vi) Inadequate fund.
(vii) Lack of access of strictly confidential information.
(viii) Lack of transport system.
(ix) Presence of wars.

CHAPTER NINE

SAMPLE, SAMPLING AND SAMPLING TECHNIQUES

Sample *is* a small part or quantity intended to show what the whole is like. **Sampling** is the process by which a representative portion of the population is selected for analysis. **Sampling Techniques** are tactics of selecting the portion of resprepresentatives.

Criteria of Selecting a Sampling Procedure

Two costs are involved in a sampling analysis. The cost of collecting the data and the cost of an incorrect inference resulting from the data. Researcher must keep in view the two causes of incorrect inferences viz., systematic bias and sampling error. A *systematic bias* results from errors in the sampling procedures, and it cannot be reduced or eliminated by increasing the sample size. At best the causes responsible for these errors can be detected and corrected.

Usually a systematic bias is the result of one or more of the following factors:

1. Inappropriate sampling frame: If the sampling frame is inappropriate i.e., a biased representation of the universe, it will result in a systematic bias.

2. Defective measuring device: If the measuring device is constantly in error, it will result in systematic bias. In survey work, systematic bias can result if the questionnaire or the interviewer is biased. Similarly, if the physical measuring device is defective there will be systematic bias in the data collected through such a measuring device.

3. Non-respondents: If we are unable to sample all the individuals initially included in the sample, there may arise a systematic bias. The reason is that in such a situation the likelihood of establishing contact or receiving a response from an individual is often correlated with the measure of what is to be estimated.

4. Indeterminacy principle: Sometimes we find that individuals act differently when kept under observation than what they do when kept in non-observed situations. For instance, if workers are aware that somebody is observing them in course of a work study on the basis of which the average length of time to complete a task will be determined and accordingly the quota will be set for piece work, they generally tend to work slowly in comparison to the speed with which they work if kept unobserved. Thus, the indeterminacy principle may also be a cause of a systematic bias.

5. Natural bias in the reporting of data: Natural bias of respondents in the reporting of data is often the cause of a systematic bias in many inquiries. There is usually a downward bias in the income data collected by government taxation department, whereas we find an upward bias in the income data collected by some social organisation. People in general understate their incomes if asked about it for tax purposes, but they overstate the same if asked for social status or their affluence. Generally in psychological surveys, people tend to give what they think is the 'correct' answer rather than revealing their true feelings.

Characteristics of a Good Sample Design
From what has been stated above, we can list down the characteristics of a good sample design as under:
    a. Sample design must result in a truly representative sample.
    b. Sample design must be such which results in a small sampling error.
    c. Sample design must be viable in the context of funds available for the research study.
    d. Sample design must be such so that systematic bias can be controlled in a better way.
    e. Sample should be such that the results of the sample study can be applied, in general, for the universe with a reasonable level of confidence.

Need for Sampling

Sampling is used in practice for a variety of reasons such as:

1. Sampling can save time and money. A sample study is usually less expensive than a census study and produces results at a relatively faster speed.
2. Sampling may enable more accurate measurements for a sample study is generally conducted by trained and experienced investigators.
3. Sampling remains the only way when population contains infinitely many members.
4. Sampling remains the only choice when a test involves the destruction of the item under study.
5. Sampling usually enables to estimate the sampling errors and, thus, assists in obtaining information concerning some characteristic of the population.

Types of sampling (sampling techniques)

They are two types or classification of sampling, as namely:

(a) Probability sampling (Have the following types):
   (i) Simple random sampling.
   (ii) Systematic sampling.
   (iii) Stratified sampling.
   (iv) Cluster sampling.

(b) Non-probability sampling (have the followings):
   (i) Purposive sampling.
   (ii) Quota sampling.
   (iii) Snowball sampling.
   (iv) Convenience sampling.
   (v) Concecutive sampling

(A)   Probability Sampling

Probabilitty sampling refers to an equal sampling technique in which data that are found can be used for generalization. Probability sampling is also known as *random sampling*. The member in this population have equal chance to be selected.

Types of probability sampling:

1. ***Simple Random Sampling:*** By definition, simple random sampling is the technique that provides an equal chance to every member in a population to be included in the study. It is the equal probability sampling method in selection. The method, which is sometimes called **randomization** is for rotary system. The method reduece any form of bias and errors is selecting samples.

2. ***Systematic Sampling:*** It is the type of sampling that involves selection of the sample randomly at regular interval from the sampling frame. This is the systematic selection of the participarts. It involves selection of each nth term where after every 3,5,7 or 10 individuals. Individuals might be selected and indicated by name or numbers. In the selection of the nth term should follow the clear interval and sample size.

3. ***Stratified Sampling:*** Is the sampling technique that involves dividing up the population into smaller groups known as **strata**. This reduce the omission of important elements. The technique have got two types:
   a) Proportional stratified sampling (This does not reflect the size)
   b) Disproportional stratified sampling (This do reflect the size).

4. ***Cluster Or Ecological Sampling:*** Involves random selection of a group and each member is the group participates in the research.   Is a frequently used method and more practicle in the sampling especially in the probability sampling. In this, the population is classified into two level: *lowest level* and *highest level*.

(B)   Non-Probability Sampling

In this type, the member in the population have no equal chance to be selected. Researcher select the sampling or sample with purpose (prior purpose). Selection is based on the personal judgement like; (i) Purposive based judgement and (ii)Accessibility based judgement. Due to being no generalisation, the method of sampling is very usefull for qualitative research.

Types of Non-Probability Sampling

1. ***Convenience Sampling:***In this, researcher selectsample because of accessibility. This is due to be easily accessed. It is probably most common in non-probability method of sampling. Involves the selection of sample according to the researcher convinience, like terms of time, money, human resources. This is commonly known as *accessial sampling.*

2. ***Concecutive Sampling:*** This is very smilar to the convinience technique where it collects individual to become the sample because of accessibilities. The researcher have to collect all the individuals who are accessible like all University students. Is useful where the population is very small then all member to be collected and at the end the researcher is able to analyze the data.

3. ***Quota Sampling:*** This is the technique that describe the sample that equivalent to technique. This have the same characteristics of the stratified sampling technique. Involves in division of individuals into small groups which are known as *quota*. Foreexample; the work hard may represent the significant characteristics of of the population. The quota can be age, economic status, level of performance, sex among others.

In this sampling technique, the researcher have to ensure equal of proportional representation of the subject in which traits are considered from the quota. Also the sampling divide the population into small group and subsection have to represent the population.

4. ***Purposive or Judgemental Sampling:*** It is judgemental or purposive sampling where by researcher believes that, the individuals have the information about the particulars. The subject is chosen to become a

sample because of specific purpose. This involves the selection of few respondents, believing that, they have the information.

5. **Snowball Sampling:** It is the sampling technique that is used in a small size of the population. Snowball sampling is also known as *Strategic sampling.* It is characterized by identified single individual (few individuals) then ask them to recommend to other individuals, who are smillar to their characteristics.

Qn. When to use probability and Non probability sampling technique?

CHAPTER TEN

REPORT PRESENTATION IN RESEARCH

Report writing or report presentation refers to the vital step as one (researcher) communicate his or her findings to other researcher or the public. This is the last step of a research. In this stage; finally, a researcher has to prepare the report of what has been done by him. Writing of report must be done with great care keeping in viewing the following:

1. **The layout of the report should be as follows:**
   (*i*) The preliminary pages,
   (*ii*) The main text and
   (*iii*) The end matter.

In its preliminary pages the report should carry title and date followed by acknowledgements and foreword. Then there should be a table of contents followed by a list of tables and list of graphs and charts, if any, given in the report.

The main text of the report should have the following parts:
 (a) *Introduction:* It should contain a clear statement of the objective of the research and an explanation of the methodology adopted in accomplishing the research. The scope of the study along with various limitations should as well be stated in this part.

(b) *Summary of findings:* After introduction there would appear a statement of findings and recommendations in non-technical language. If the findings are extensive, they should be summarized.

(c) *Main report:* The main body of the report should be presented in logical sequence and broken-down into readily identifiable sections.

(d) *Conclusion:* Towards the end of the main text, researcher should again put down the results of his research clearly and precisely. In fact, it is the final summing up.

At the end of the report, appendices should be enlisted in respect of all technical data. Bibliography, i.e., list of books, journals, reports, etc., consulted, should also be given in the end. Index should also be given specially in a published research report.

2. Report should be written in a concise and objective style in simple language avoiding vague expressions such as 'it seems,' 'there may be', and the like.

3. Charts and illustrations in the main report should be used only if they present the information more clearly and forcibly.

4. Calculated 'confidence limits' must be mentioned and the various constraints experienced in conducting research operations may as well be stated.

Qn: Discuss for the Significance of Report Writing

Different Steps in Writing Report
Research reports are the product of slow, painstaking, accurate inductive work. The usual steps involved in writing report are:
   (a) Logical analysis of the subject-matter,
   (b) Preparation of the final outline,
   (c) Preparation of the rough draft,
   (d) Rewriting and polishing,
   (c) Preparation of the final bibliography and
   (f) Writing the final draft.

Logical analysis of the subject matter: It is the first step which is primarily concerned with the development of a subject. There are two ways in which to develop a subject
   (a) Logically and

(b) Chronologically.

The logical development is made on the basis of mental connections and associations between the one thing and another by means of analysis. Logical treatment often consists in developing the material from the simple possible to the most complex structures. Chronological development is based on a connection or sequence in time or occurrence. The directions for doing or making something usually follow the chronological order.

Preparation of the final outline: It is the next step in writing the research report "Outlines are the framework upon which long written works are constructed. They are an aid to the logical organization of the material and a reminder of the points to be stressed in the report."

Preparation of the rough draft: This follows the logical analysis of the subject and the preparation *of the rough draft:* This follows the logical analysis of the subject and the preparation of the final outline. Such a step is of utmost importance for the researcher now sits to write down what he has done in the context of his research study. He will write down the procedure adopted by him in collecting the material for his study along with various limitations faced by him, the technique of analysis adopted by him, the broad findings and generalizations and the various suggestions he wants to offer regarding the problem concerned.

Rewriting and polishing of the rough draft: This step happens to be most difficult part of all formal writing. Usually this step requires more time than the writing of the rough draft. The careful revision makes the difference between a mediocre and a good piece of writing. While rewriting and polishing, one should check the report for weaknesses in logical development or presentation.

The researcher should also "see whether or not the material, as it is presented, has unity and cohesion; does the report stand upright and firm and exhibit a definite pattern, like a marble arch? Or does it resemble an old wall of moldering cement and loose brick." In addition the researcher should give due attention to the fact that in his rough draft he has been consistent or not. He should check the mechanics of writing—grammar, spelling and usage.

Preparation of the final bibliography*:* Next in order comes the task of the preparation of the final bibliography. The bibliography, which is generally appended to the research report, is a list of books in some way pertinent to the research which has been done. It should contain all those works which the researcher has consulted. The bibliography should be arranged alphabetically and may be divided into two parts; the first part may contain the names of books and pamphlets, and the second part may contain the names of magazine and newspaper articles.

Generally, this pattern of bibliography is considered convenient and satisfactory from the point of view of reader, though it is not the only way of presenting bibliography. The entries in bibliography should be made adopting the following order:

For books and pamphlets the order may be as under: 1. Name of author, last name first. 2. Title, underlined to indicate italics. 3. Place, publisher, and date of publication. 4. Number of volumes.

For magazines and newspapers the order may be as under: 1. Name of the author, last name first. 2. Title of article, in quotation marks. 3. Name of periodical, underlined to indicate italics. 4. The volume or volume and number. 5. The date of the issue. 6. The pagination.

Writing the final draft: This constitutes the last step. The final draft should be written in a concise and objective style and in simple language, avoiding vague expressions such as "it seems", "there may be", and the like ones. While writing the final draft, the researcher must avoid abstract terminology and technical jargon. Illustrations and examples based on common experiences must be incorporated in the final draft as they happen to be most effective in communicating the research findings to others. A research report should not be dull, but must enthuse people and maintain interest and must show originality.

Layout of the Research Report

Anybody, who is reading the research report, must necessarily be conveyed enough about the study so that he can place it in its general scientific context, judge the adequacy of its methods and thus, form an opinion of how seriously the findings are to be taken. For this purpose there is the need of proper layout of the report.

The layout of the report means as to what the research report should contain. A comprehensive layout of the research report should comprise:
    (A) Preliminary pages;
    (B) The main text; and
    (C) The end matter.
    (A) Preliminary Pages

(A) *Preliminary pages*

In this, the report should carry a *title and date,* followed by acknowledgements in the form of 'Preface' or 'Foreword'. Then there should be a *table of contents* followed by *list of tables and illustrations* so that the decision-maker or anybody interested in reading the report can easily locate the required information in the report.

(B) *Main Text*

The main text provides the complete outline of the research report along with all details. Title of the research study is repeated at the top of the first page of the main text and then follows the other details on pages numbered consecutively, beginning with the second page. Each main section of the report should begin on a new page. The main text of the report should have the following sections:
    (i) Introduction;
    (ii) Statement of findings and recommendations;
    (iii) The results;
    (iv) The implications drawn from the results; and
    (v) The summary.

(i) *Introduction:* The purpose of introduction is to introduce the research project to the readers. It should contain a clear statement of the objectives of research i.e., enough background should be given to make clear to the reader why the problem was considered worth investigating. A brief summary of other relevant research may also be stated so that the present study can be seen in that context. The hypotheses of study, if any, and the definitions of the major concepts employed in the study should be explicitly stated in the introduction of the report.

The methodology adopted in conducting the study must be fully explained. The scientific reader would like to know in detail about such thing: How was the study carried out? What was its basic design? If the study was an experimental one, then what were the experimental manipulations? If the data were collected by means of questionnaires or interviews, then exactly what questions were asked (The questionnaire or interview schedule is usually given in an appendix)?

If measurements were based on observation, then what instructions were given to the observers? Regarding the sample used in the study the reader should be told: Who were the subjects? How many were there? How were they selected? All these questions are crucial for estimating the probable limits of generalizability of the findings. The statistical analysis adopted must also be clearly stated. In addition to all this, the scope of the study should be stated and the boundary lines be demarcated. The various limitations, under which the research project was completed, must also be narrated.

(ii) *Statement of findings and recommendations:* After introduction, the research report must contain a statement of findings and recommendations in non-technical language so that it can be easily understood by all concerned. If the findings happen to be extensive, at this point they should be put in the summarised form.

(iii) Results: A detailed presentation of the findings of the study, with supporting data in the form of tables and charts together with a validation of results, is the next step in writing the main text of the report. This

71

generally comprises the main body of the report, extending over several chapters. The result section of the report should contain statistical summaries and reductions of the data rather than the raw data. All the results should be presented in logical sequence and splitted into readily identifiable sections.

All relevant results must find a place in the report. But how one is to decide about what is relevant is the basic question. Quite often guidance comes primarily from the research problem and from the hypotheses, if any, with which the study was concerned. But ultimately the researcher must rely on his own judgments in deciding the outline of his report. "Nevertheless, it is still necessary that he states clearly the problem with which he was concerned, the procedure by which he worked on the problem, the conclusions at which he arrived, and the bases for his conclusions."

(iv) *Implications of the results:* Toward the end of the main text, the researcher should again put down the results of his research clearly and precisely. He should, state the implications that flow from the results of the study, for the general reader is interested in the implications for understanding the human behaviour. Such implications may have three aspects as stated below:

> (a) A statement of the inferences drawn from the present study which may be expected to apply in similar circumstances.
> (b) The conditions of the present study which may limit the extent of legitimate generalizations of the inferences drawn from the study.
> (c) The relevant questions that still remain unanswered or new questions raised by the study along with suggestions for the kind of research that would provide answers for them.

(v) *Summary:* It has become customary to conclude the research report with a very brief summary, resting in brief the research problem, the methodology, the major findings and the major conclusions drawn from the research results.

(C) *End Matter*

At the end of the report, appendices should be enlisted in respect of all technical data such as questionnaires, sample information, mathematical derivations and the like ones. Bibliography of sources consulted should also be given. Index (an alphabetical listing of names, places and topics along with the numbers of the pages in a book or report on which they are mentioned or discussed) should invariably be given at the end of the report. The value of index lies in the fact that it works as a guide to the reader for the contents in the report.

Types of Research Reports

Research reports vary greatly in length and type. For instance, business firms prefer reports in the letter form, just one or two pages in length. Banks, insurance organisations and financial institutions are generally fond of the short balance-sheet type of tabulation for their annual reports to their customers and shareholders.

Mathematicians prefer to write the results of their investigations in the form of algebraic notations. Chemists report their results in symbols and formulae. Students of literature usually write long reports presenting the critical analysis of some writer or period or the like with a liberal use of quotations from the works of the author under discussion.

In the field of education and psychology, the favourite form is the report on the results of experimentation accompanied by the detailed statistical tabulations. Clinical psychologists and social pathologists frequently find it necessary to make use of the case-history form. News items in the daily papers are also forms of report writing.

They represent firsthand on the scene accounts of the events described or compilations of interviews with persons who were on the scene. In such reports the first paragraph usually contains the important information in detail and the succeeding paragraphs contain material which is progressively less and less important.

Book-reviews which analyze the content of the book and report on the author's intentions, his success or failure in achieving his aims, his language, his style, scholarship, bias or his point of view. Such reviews also happen to be a kind of short report. The reports prepared by governmental bureaus, special commissions, and similar other organisations are generally very comprehensive reports on the issues involved. Such reports are usually considered as important research products. Similarly Ph.D. theses and dissertations are also a form of report-writing, usually completed by students in academic institutions.

The above narration throws light on the fact that the results of a research investigation can be presented in a number of ways viz., a technical report, a popular report, an article, a monograph or at times even in the form of oral presentation. Which method(s) of presentation to be used in a particular study depends on the circumstances under which the study arose and the nature of the results. A *technical report* is used whenever a full written report of the study is required whether for recordkeeping or for public dissemination. A *popular report* is used if the research results have policy implications.

The following are few Details about the Two Types of Reports:
(A) Technical Report: In the technical report the main emphasis is on
  (i) The methods employed,
  (ii) Assumptions made in the course of the study,
  (iii) The detailed presentation of the findings including their limitations and supporting data.

(B) Popular Report: The popular report is one which gives emphasis on simplicity and attractiveness. The simplification should be sought through clear writing, minimization of technical, particularly mathematical, details and liberal use of charts and diagrams. Attractive layout along with large print, many subheadings, even an occasional cartoon now and then is another characteristic feature of the popular report. Besides, in such a report emphasis is given on practical aspects and policy implications.

Importance of Research Report Rriting:

(i) It exposes the problems which have bee researched and their implication.

(ii) It fully presents the outcome of data collected of the research.

(iii) It enterprete the data obtained from the field.

(iv) It provides the data around the problems investigated.

The Report format in asummary way:

Chapter 1, 2 and 3 are the main chapters for the research proposal:

(i) Preliminary information

(ii) The main body

(iii) Recommendation

Features of Research Report

(i) Must have a focus.

(ii) Must have a good organisation.

(iii) Must be characterized by integration.

Uses of Research Outputs and Recommendation:

(i) Improve knowledge of the people.

(ii) Assists in finding problems inflicting societies.

(iii) To improve economic and social activities.

(iv) Result to exploitation of formely untrapped resources.

(v) Results in variates of communities needs.

(vi) Solution are usefull in protecting and conserving the environment.

(vii) Used in formulation of government policies.

CHAPTER ELEVEN

FIELD TECHNIQUES AND RESEARCH PROPOSAL

Field research is the branch of field work which deals with problem solving and geographical investigation as well as promoting further research for the problem to be tackled by another approch. Field techniques involves field study, field excusion and field work.

Field Study

It is any learning activities carried by individual or group of individul outside the classroom. It is where a person is physically involved in observation, recording, interpreting and writing the report on all observed facts in a particular field. It is also refered to *field technique* or *study tour.*

Stages involved in field study (an example of study tour to academic intitutions):

1. *Preparation:*Teacher's preparation (planning by the teacher) and Students' preparation.

2. *Application for paying a vist*: application letter to inform or ask for a permission:
   a) To the school or college administration.
   b) To the parents if possible
   c) To the site expected to be researched and visted.

3. *Transport preparation*: travelling preparation.

4. *Arrival and data taking:* taking data through noting what observed in the field.

Advantages of Field Study
   a) Students arose interests in a particular aspect due awakening to further deeper study.

b) Develop skills of writing, recording, interpretation, observation, drawing sketch and assessment to the students.
c) Promote more creativity of students among others.

Disadvantages of Field Study
a) The method is time consuming in preparation, recording and interpretation.
b) It is very expensive in term of transport and accomodation
c) The method can distort the academic institution time table
d) Data may be merely collected and maps and descriptive diagrams drawn with no attempt to analyse the findings.
e) The physical environment tend to dominate the environment.

Field Excursion
In this, learners vist the site and report all aspects they observed on the way and at the site.

Field Work
It is the science of selecting, Observing, measuring, evaluating and reporting on geographical phenomena in a specific area.

Branches of Field Work:
(i) Field excursion: In this, learners vist the site and report all aspects they observed on the way and at the site.

(ii) Field study (tour): It is any learning activities carried by individual or group of individul outside the classroom. It is where a person is physically involved in observation, recording, interpreting and writing the report on all observed facts in a particular field.

(iii) Feasibility study: This seeks to establish the livehood of a proposal project being beneficial and successful to the community in general. Feasibility studies are often conducted by a team of expert traced in different subjects.

Objectives and iportance of Field Work

The field work have the following objectives:

a) Enables researcher to relate documents and other geographical information.

b) Provide students with an opportunity to develop interdependence among students with common interest.

c) Enable students to develop independent judgement of real life in relation with human and physical geography.

d) Influence scientific methods of enquiry to the students when they become more critical in their assessment (and gives a student a sense of personal achievement).

Research Propasal

By definition, research proposal refers to a descriptive plan, which is to be followed in carring out a particlar research or study. It is also defined as a plan of action to be followed in the particular study or research.

Research proposal should be dominated by the use of *future tense*, since it is a plan that not yet done. A good research proposal should have to answer the following questions:

o What do you want to do?
o How much will it cost?
o How much time will it take?
o What difference will the research make to the society or nation?
o What has already been done in the area of your the research?
o How do you plan to do it?
o How will the results be evaluated?

Types of research proposals

Research proposals involves five types: solicited research proposal, pre research proposal, continuation research proposal, unsoliciting research proposal and renewal (competing) research proposal.

1. *Solicited Research Proposal:* it is a research proposal submitted in response to a specific solicitation issued by a sponsor. It is usually specific

in its requirement regarding to format and technical content, and may stipulate certain terms and conditions.

2. *Unsolcited Research Proposal*: it is a proposal that submitted to a sponsor which has not issued a specific solicitation but is believed by the ivestigators to have interest in the subject.

3. *Pre Proposal:* this is the proposal required when a sponsor wishes to minimize an applicant's effort in preparing full proposal.

4. *Continuation Research Proposal:* it is a research proposal which confirms the original proposal and funding requirements of a multi-year project for which the sponsor has already provided funding for an initial periods normally one year continued support. It is usually contigent on satisfactory work progress and availability of funds.

5. *Renewal Research Proposal:* it is a proposal which requests for continued support from the sponsor's view point for an existing project that about to reach an end of the contract.

Function and Importance of Research Proposal:
1. It enables the researcher and research assistants to know how long the research will take to be completed.
2. It acts as the guide for general strategies to be undertaken.
3. It enables the researcher to know the cost of the research
4. It helps the researcher to think over important issues about the study, such as how to collect data who will provide the data and where the information is available.
5. It helps the researcher in evaluating the study through looking at the difficulties which are likely to be involved and making necessary modifications.

Format of Research Proposal
Research proposal format is the general patterns of the organisation and arrangements of the study that involves the following parts or stages:

1. *Preliminary part:* this includes title of the study, name of the researcher, abstract, table of contents, year of study and list of tables.

2. *Main body:* basically is made up:
   o Chapter one is the background of the research problems. Normally it contain sub-parts like introduction, statement of the problem, objectives of the study, research questions or hypotheses, scope of the study, significances of the study, limitations of the study and delimitation of the study.
   o Chapter two is literature review, which is all about reviewing of related literatures being theoretically, impirical review and research gaps to be filled.
   o Chapter three is research methodology which complise of population, sample, instrunments of data collection, proposed data analysis, methods to be employed and time frame.

2. *Back Page (end matters):* the back pages of research proposal consists of important supportive attachment like tentative budget, data collection tools.

Field Research Strategies

TRIAL QUESTIONS

(1)   Answer the following questions:
    a) What is research?
    b) Describe the basic steps for carrying out a research.
    c) Discuss the uses of research outputs and recommendations
    d) Differentiate a null from a positive hypothesis
    e) Why do we need a research in our daily lives?

(2)   Differentiate by giving examples the following terms:
    a) Closed and open questionnaires
    b) Structured and Non structured interview
    c) Participant and Non participant observation

(3)   What circumstances would you decide to sample your research participants using probability or non probability techniques?

(4)   Draw some examples from your research knowledge, show how all the steps in research process are interconnected to form a coherent research enterprese.

(5)   The term research is widely used by different people to give the meaning of it. Use examples from your research knowledge to differentiate proper reseaech from what is not. Discuss altleast five characteristics that make a research as science.

(6)   What are the uses or importance, advantages and disadvantages of research hypothesis.

(7)   Write short notes on:
    a) Design of the research project;
    b) Expost facto research;
    c) Motivation in research;
    d) Objectives of research;

e) Criteria of good research;

f) Research and scientific method.

(8) "Empirical research in Tanzania in particular creates so many problems for the researchers". State the problems that are usually faced by such researchers.

(9) "Creative management, whether in public administration or private industry, depends on methods of inquiry that maintain objectivity, clarity, accuracy and consistency". Discuss this statement and examine the significance of research".

(10) "Research is much concerned with proper fact finding, analysis and evaluation." Do you agree with this statement? Give reasons in support of your answer.

(11) It is often said that there is not a proper link between some of the activities under way in the world of academics and in most business in our country. Account for this state of affairs and give suggestions for improvement.

(12) Describe fully the techniques of defining a research problem.

(13) What is research problem? Define the main issues which should receive the attention of the researcher in formulating the research problem.

(14) What is the necessity of defining a research problem? Explain.

(15) Write short notes on:
(a) Experience survey; (b) Pilot survey; (c) Components of a research problem; (d) Rephrasing the research problem.

(16) What do you mean by 'Sample Design'? What points should be taken into consideration by a researcher in developing a sample design for this research project.

(17) How would you differentiate between simple random sampling and complex random sampling designs? Explain clearly giving examples.

(18) Why probability sampling is generally preferred in comparison to non-probability sampling? Explain the procedure of selecting a simple random sample.

(19) Under what circumstances stratified random sampling design is considered appropriate? How would you select such sample? Explain by means of an example.

(20) *Distinguish between:*
    (a) Restricted and unrestricted sampling;
    (b) Convenience and purposive sampling;
    (c) Systematic and stratified sampling;
    (d) Cluster and area sampling.

(21) *Under what circumstances would you recommend:*
    (a) A probability sample?
    (b) A non-probability sample?
    (c) A stratified sample?
    (d) A cluster sample?

(22) Explain and illustrate the procedure of selecting a random sample. "A systematic bias results from errors in the sampling procedures". What do you mean by such a systematic bias? Describe the important causes responsible for such a bias.

(23) The following are the number of departmental stores in 10 cities: 35, 27, 24, 32, 42, 30, 34, 40, 29 and 38. If you want to select a sample of 15 stores using cities as clusters and selecting within clusters proportional to size, how many stores from each city should be chosen? (use a starting point)

BIBLIOGRAPHY

APE NETWORK, (2008): *Ordinary level Geography review:* Dar es Salaam. APE network Publisher.

Furguson, A. G and Ngau, P. M, (1981): *Field and Data Analysis in Geograph.* Nairobi: Macmillan.

Jack R.F and Norman E. W, (2000): *How to Design and Evaluate Research in Education.*

Kothari C.R, (2004). *Research Methodology:* Method and Techniques 2nd Ed: New Delhi, New age International Publishers

Pritchard J. M, (1990). *Practical geography for Africa:* Hong Kong. Longman Group (FE) Ltd.

Field Research Strategies